THIS BOOK BELONGS TO:

_____

Adventure Journal

ADVENTURE AWAITS

CREATED BY KAREN STOTT
ILLUSTRATED BY JORDANNE VANWERT

INTENTIONAL HOME ®

Adventures with Archer ™
Archer's Adventure Journal ™
Copyright Intentional Home 2015 -2017
This title is available on our website www.adventureswitharcher.com

Created by Karen Stott
Cover Illustration by Jordanne VanWert
Editing Team: Janice Nielsen

Bible verses used throughout:

HOW TO USE THE JOURNAL

— TODAY'S VERSE IS: —

The goal of this section is to help children memorize scripture. Have your child copy the verse above and write it here.

— I AM THANKFUL FOR: —

My friends & my stuffed animal

— I AM PRAYING FOR: —

That no one gets hurt at the game, and for my cousin's broken arm

— WHAT I LIKED ABOUT TODAY: —

I got picked to be the class line leader

— WHAT WAS HARD ABOUT TODAY: —

I didn't get a good grade & the baby gets more attention than me

— HOW CAN I SHOW LOVE? —

I can help with dinner, give hugs & clean the baby's toys up

— TODAY I FEEL: —

A little nervous about going to a new school

— WHAT DOES GOD SAY ABOUT HOW I FEEL? —

This section can be as in-depth or as simple, as you like. You can do character studies, ask them what God is telling them, or use the feelings guide in the back. Just use this space to help them connect with God where they are.

Our Story

Archer's Adventure Journal is a happy accident of divine nature. I never had any intention of designing children's journals, but God always seems to have plans that perfectly interject right into our path. Sometimes, without realizing it, we find ourselves doing something we never would've imagined, yet we know deep down it is exactly what God had planned for us all along. And that's where I find myself today.

Shortly after I released our first Intentional Home Journal for women, my kids started begging me for one of their own. And since I have boys in the mix, they wanted one that wasn't covered in hand-painted peonies. That's when God started writing a plan on all of our hearts to create a journal specifically for kids to discover God's Word for themselves. Each of my children designed their own *ideal* pages, questions, and layouts. What you see in this journal is a collaboration of a God-seed thought, my children's hearts, and a lot of dreaming, implementing, and honing from Isaac and me.

Soon after we started the project, my creative heart began dreaming of little friends who could join our children on this adventure of journaling and exploring the Bible. I reached out to my incredibly talented friend, Jordanne, and together, we dreamed up Archer, the fox, and his band of friends.

As I type this story for you today, I'm simply overwhelmed with God's goodness and graceful intervention into "our story." His ways truly are the best ways. When our first copy of Archer's Adventure Journal got delivered to our door, my kids ripped open the box and immediately began arguing over who got to write in it first. My mistake, I should've ordered two! We all got a good laugh, and it became very apparent that these are to be treasured as individual sacred spaces for our kids, much like our own prayer journals. My hope and prayer for you and yours is that your kids will experience the same ripping-open enthusiasm to get into God's Word and start a conversation with Him, just as mine did.. Without the arguing part, of course! LOL!

We hope that Archer and his friends become a fun invitation for you and your child to explore hearts, truths, and how the Bible actually applies to our lives. At the end of the journal, you will have a priceless book that your child has written about their lives, and what they learned about the Lord. I can't think of a better treasure to keep (and pass down) than a collection of their own thoughts, prayers, and daily happenings.

Thank you so much for joining the Adventure!

Much love from our family to yours,
Isaac, Karen, Ava, Isaiah & Logan Stott

WWW.KARENSTOTT.COM

Letter to Parents & Teachers

Thank you so much for taking this step of faith with us to help the children in our lives cultivate a love for God's Word and journaling His voice. We hope and pray it's a huge blessing to all of you!

As you begin to explore the journal with your child, we want to reiterate that the heart behind this project is to cultivate a love, and a habit, in our children to get in God's Word daily. We want to give them space to pause and reflect on His goodness and His voice. We want to help them become intentional about quietly spending a bit of time with Him every day.

One of our biggest prayers is that children will learn that the Bible is more than just fun stories. It is alive and true and applicable to how they feel, and what they are going through right now. It wasn't until my early twenties that I started to grasp that God's Word was actually applicable and had lessons and truths that could help me navigate through my life's circumstances. I had known stories about heroes in the Bible, but I had never been introduced to the lessons behind the stories, or how God showed Himself to these men and women. I want to help the next generation have a better understanding of the Bible, what it tells us about God's character, and how it can truly help them in their everyday lives.

Depending on the age of the children you are working with, your quiet times are going to look very different. If you have a four or five year old, you may need to ask them questions each day and write in the answers for them while they color along. If you have a ten year old, you may want to explore the Bible verses more with them, and dive further into the stories and truths that can be applied. There are no rules here, we just want to be a guide into exploring God and His Word so that our children can begin to build their own faith.

One of my favorite parts of the journal is the Feelings Guide in the back. This is something that I created to give children a quick reference to a Bible verse that can help them, no matter how they are feeling or what they are going through. This guide is specifically helpful for the last question of the daily pages, "What does God say about how I feel?" It helps your kids connect the dots from how they might be feeling to a Bible verse that addresses that exact feeling. Once they find an applicable verse, they can write it in the last box at the bottom of the page. This isn't a hard-and-fast rule though, it's meant to invite them to explore what God is saying about their situation, whether that's from the Bible or prayer. My ten year old daughter told me a few weeks ago that she doesn't use the Feelings Guide to answer the last daily question... " I just write what God's telling me, Mama." Wow! "Okay, PERFECT!" I told her. I love how these journals have enough structure to help children in their quiet times, but also give them freedom to make their time with God their own.

Like I previously mentioned, this journal is meant to be a guide to help them deepen their own relationship with Jesus, not a rule book. So please feel free to use it how God leads, and how it best fits your family or classroom. I hope that through the years of journaling with Archer, our kids will be able to look back through their journals and see all the ways God has been faithful in their lives. What an incredible legacy of faith you are helping them cultivate! High fives to you!

If you have any suggestions, testimonies, or things you'd like to see added in the future, I'd love to hear from you! Please email me directly at Karen@KarenStott.com. We also LOVE seeing Archer in action. Please feel free to share photos and stories of your family using Archer on social media. If you tag us @AdventureswithArcher, and #ArchersAdventureJournal, we will see your posts, and maybe even share them on our page!

From our family to yours, thank you so much for your support. We hope and pray that you enjoy the adventure!

Karen Stott

All About Me

My Favorite:

Animal is _____

Color is _____

Movie is _____

Book is _____

Song is _____

I Am:

I am _____ years old

I am _____ inches tall

I am in _____ grade

I show people I love them by:

I know someone loves me if they:

My favorite things to do for fun are:

If I could go anywhere in the world,
I would go to:

When I grow up I want to:

My favorite place is:

Why?

Look How Big My Hand Is

TRACE YOUR CHILD'S HAND, OR DIP IT IN PAINT OR INK

#ArchersAdventureJournal

Meet Archer

/arCHer/

noun: a person who shoots with a bow and arrows, especially at a target

HI NEW FRIEND!

I AM SO EXCITED THAT WE GET TO SPEND SOME TIME TOGETHER!
WE ARE GOING TO HAVE SO MUCH FUN
SHARING ADVENTURES, PRAYING TOGETHER, AND
LEARNING WHAT GOD AND THE BIBLE SAY ABOUT YOU!

ARE YOU EXCITED TO GET STARTED? ME TOO! LET'S TRY TO SPEND A
FEW MINUTES TOGETHER EVERY DAY. IS THAT OKAY WITH YOU?
IT WILL BE SO MUCH FUN TO FOLLOW ALONG ON EACH OTHER'S
ADVENTURES, DON'T YOU THINK?

IF YOU JOURNAL EVERY DAY, AT THE END OF THIS BOOK YOU WILL
HAVE WRITTEN AN AMAZING STORY ABOUT YOUR LIFE! I HOPE AND
PRAY THAT OUR ADVENTURES WILL HELP YOU USE GOD'S WORD AS
YOUR COMPASS, AND HIS PURPOSES AS YOUR TARGET.

GOD IS GOING TO DO GREAT THINGS IN OUR TIME TOGETHER!

~ Archer

Like arrows in
the hands of a
warrior are
children born in
one's youth.

PSALM 127 : 4

Name Archer's Friends

TATUM

BRYANTHAYDEN

MARFTY

TYLER

CORA

I AM Statements

These statements are paraphrased from their original Bible verses to create simple I AM statements for easy learning. Please see the Bible verse referenced to read the completed verse.

I am God's child. Galatians 3:26

I am Jesus' friend. John 15:15

I am a whole new person with a whole new life.
2 Corinthians 5:17

I am totally and completely forgiven. 1 John 1:9

I am created in God's likeness. Ephesians 4:24

I am spiritually alive. Ephesians 2:5

I am a citizen of heaven. Philippians 3:20

I am God's messenger to the world. Acts 1:8

I am God's disciple-maker. Matthew 28:19

I am the salt of the earth. Matthew 5:13

I am the light of the world. Matthew 5:14

How Do I Recognize The Voices I Hear?
(based on the characters of God & Satan displayed in scripture)

God's Voice:	Satan's Voice:
Calms you	Stresses you
Comforts you	Worries you
Convicts you	Condemns you
Encourages you	Discourages you
Brings peace to you	Confuses you
Leads you	Pushes you
Reassures you	Scares you
Stills you	Rushes you

I AM

(paraphrase continued, see references for actual verses)

I am complete in Him Who is the Head of all principality and power. Colossians 2:10

I am alive with Christ. Ephesians 2:5

I am free from the law of sin and death. Romans 8:2

I am far from oppression, and fear does not come near me. Isaiah 54:14

I am born of God, and the evil one does not touch me. 1 John 5:18

I am holy and without blame before Him in love. Ephesians 1:4, 1 Peter 1:16

I have the peace of God that passes all understanding. Philippians 4:7

I have the Greater One living in me; greater is He Who is in me than He who is in the world. 1 John 4:4

I have received the spirit of wisdom and revelation in the knowledge of Jesus, the eyes of my understanding being enlightened. Ephesians 1:17-18

I have no lack, for my God supplies all of my need according to His riches in glory by Christ Jesus. Philippians 4:19

I can quench all the fiery darts of the wicked one with my shield of faith. Ephesians 6:16

I can do all things through Christ Jesus. Philippians 4:13

I am God's workmanship, created in Christ to do good works. Ephesians 2:10

I am a doer of the Word and blessed in my actions. James 1:22, 25

I am more than a conqueror through Him Who loves me. Romans 8:37

I am an overcomer by the blood of the Lamb and the word of my testimony. Revelation 12:11

I am part of a chosen generation, a royal priesthood, a holy nation, a purchased people. 1 Peter 2:9

I am the righteousness of God in Jesus Christ.   2 Corinthians 5:21

I am the temple of the Holy Spirit; I am not my own. 1 Corinthians 6:19

I AM
(paraphrase continued, see references for actual verses)

I am the head and not the tail; I am above only and not beneath. Deuteronomy 28:13

I am the light of the world. Matthew 5:14

I am His elect, full of mercy, kindness, humility, and longsuffering.   Romans 8:33, Colossians 3:12

I am forgiven of all my sins and washed in the Blood. Ephesians 1:7

I am redeemed from the curse of sin, sickness, and poverty. Deuteronomy 28:15-68, Galatians 3:13

I am firmly rooted, built up, established in my faith and overflowing with gratitude.Colossians 2:7

I am called of God to be the voice of His praise. 2 Timothy 1:9, Psalm 66:8

I am healed by the stripes of Jesus. 1 Peter 2:24, Isaiah 53:5

I am raised up with Christ and seated in Heavenly places. Ephesians 2:6, Colossians 2:12

I am greatly loved by God. Romans 1:7, Ephesians, 2:4, Colossians 3:12, 1 Thessalonians 1:4

I am strengthened with all might according to His glorious power. Colossians 1:11

I am submitted to God, and the devil flees from me because I resist him in the Name of Jesus. James 4:7

I press on toward the goal to win the prize to which God in Christ Jesus is calling us upward. Philippians 3:14

For God has not given us a spirit of fear, but of power, love, and a sound mind. 2 Timothy 1:7

Things you said

_____

_____

_____

_____

_____

_____

_____

_____

_____

_____

_____

_____

_____

_____

USE THIS PAGE TO WRITE DOWN FUN & CUTE THINGS YOUR CHILD SAYS

#ArchersAdventureJournal

Look What God Did

_____

_____

_____

_____

_____

_____

_____

_____

_____

_____

_____

_____

_____

_____

_____

_____

USE THIS SPACE TO WRITE DOWN ANSWERED PRAYERS

A Letter For You

_____

_____

_____

_____

_____

_____

_____

_____

_____

_____

_____

_____

_____

_____

USE THESE PAGES TO WRITE LETTERS TO YOUR CHILD

A Letter For You

_____

_____

_____

_____

_____

_____

_____

_____

_____

_____

_____

_____

_____

_____

_____

USE THESE PAGES TO WRITE LETTERS TO YOUR CHILD

Encouraging Words

Encouraging Words

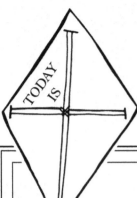

You shall love your neighbor as yourself.
MATTHEW 22:39

This week's verse is :

I am thankful for :

I am praying for :

What I liked about today :

What was hard about today :

How can I show love today?

Today I feel :

What does God say about how I feel?

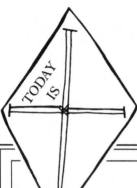

TODAY IS

You shall love your neighbor as yourself.
MATTHEW 22:39

This week's verse is :

I am thankful for :

I am praying for :

What I liked about today :

What was hard about today :

How can I show love today?

Today I feel :

What does God say about how I feel?

17

You shall love your neighbor as yourself.
MATTHEW 22:39

This week's verse is :

I am thankful for :

I am praying for :

What I liked about today :

What was hard about today :

How can I show love today?

Today I feel :

What does God say about how I feel?

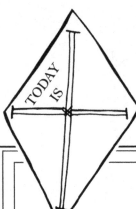

You shall love your neighbor as yourself.
MATTHEW 22:39

This week's verse is :

I am thankful for :

I am praying for :

What I liked about today :

What was hard about today :

How can I show love today?

Today I feel :

What does God say about how I feel?

#ArchersAdventureJournal

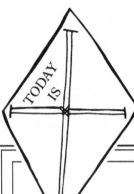

You shall love your neighbor as yourself.
MATTHEW 22:39

This week's verse is :

I am thankful for :

I am praying for :

What I liked about today :

What was hard about today :

How can I show love today?

Today I feel :

What does God say about how I feel?

What did this week's verse mean to you?

_____

_____

_____

_____

_____

_____

_____

What was one of your favorite moments this week?

_____

_____

_____

_____

_____

_____

_____

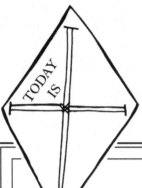

I am the good shepherd.
JOHN 10:11

This week's verse is :

I am thankful for :

I am praying for :

What I liked about today :

What was hard about today :

How can I show love today?

Today I feel :

What does God say about how I feel?

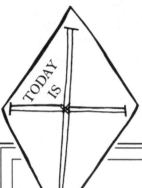

I am the good shepherd.
JOHN 10:11

This week's verse is :

I am thankful for :

I am praying for :

What I liked about today :

What was hard about today :

How can I show love today?

Today I feel :

What does God say about how I feel?

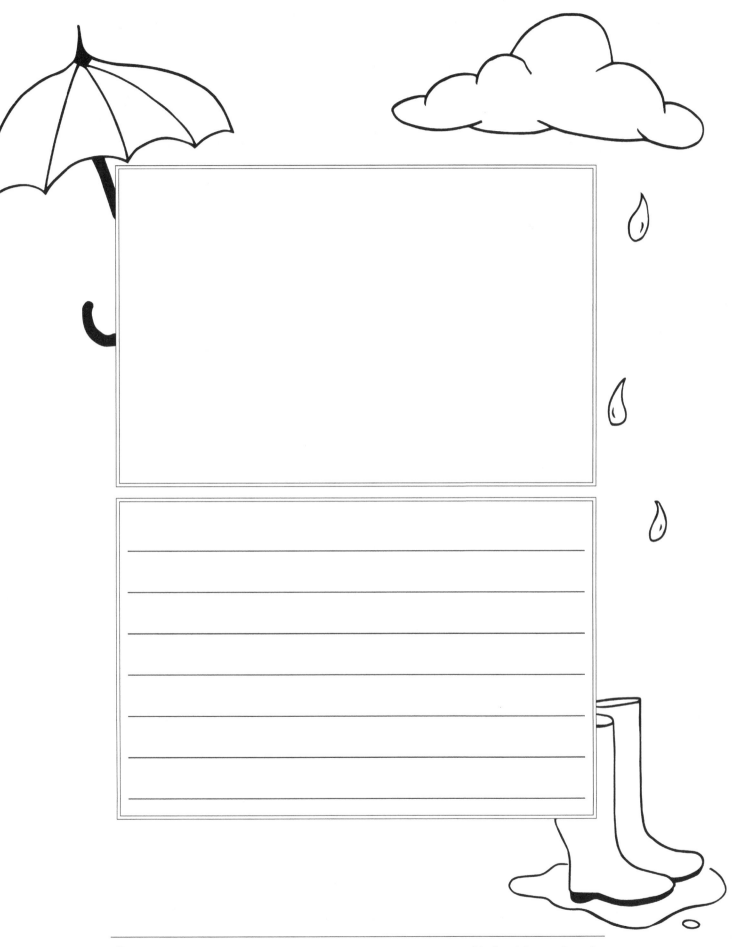

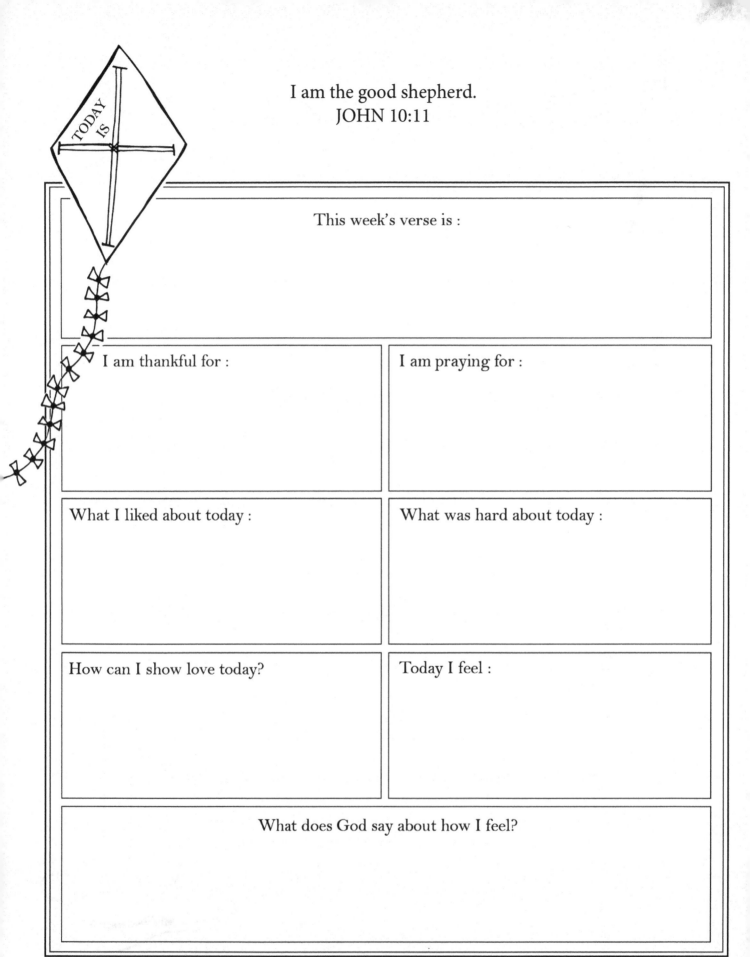

I am the good shepherd.
JOHN 10:11

TODAY IS

This week's verse is :

I am thankful for :

I am praying for :

What I liked about today :

What was hard about today :

How can I show love today?

Today I feel :

What does God say about how I feel?

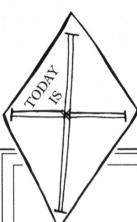

I am the good shepherd.
JOHN 10:11

This week's verse is :

I am thankful for :

I am praying for :

What I liked about today :

What was hard about today :

How can I show love today?

Today I feel :

What does God say about how I feel?

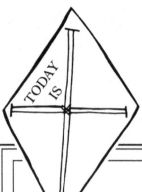

TODAY IS

I am the good shepherd.
JOHN 10:11

This week's verse is :

I am thankful for :

I am praying for :

What I liked about today :

What was hard about today :

How can I show love today?

Today I feel :

What does God say about how I feel?

What did this week's verse mean to you?

_____

_____

_____

_____

_____

_____

What was one of your favorite moments this week?

_____

_____

_____

_____

_____

_____

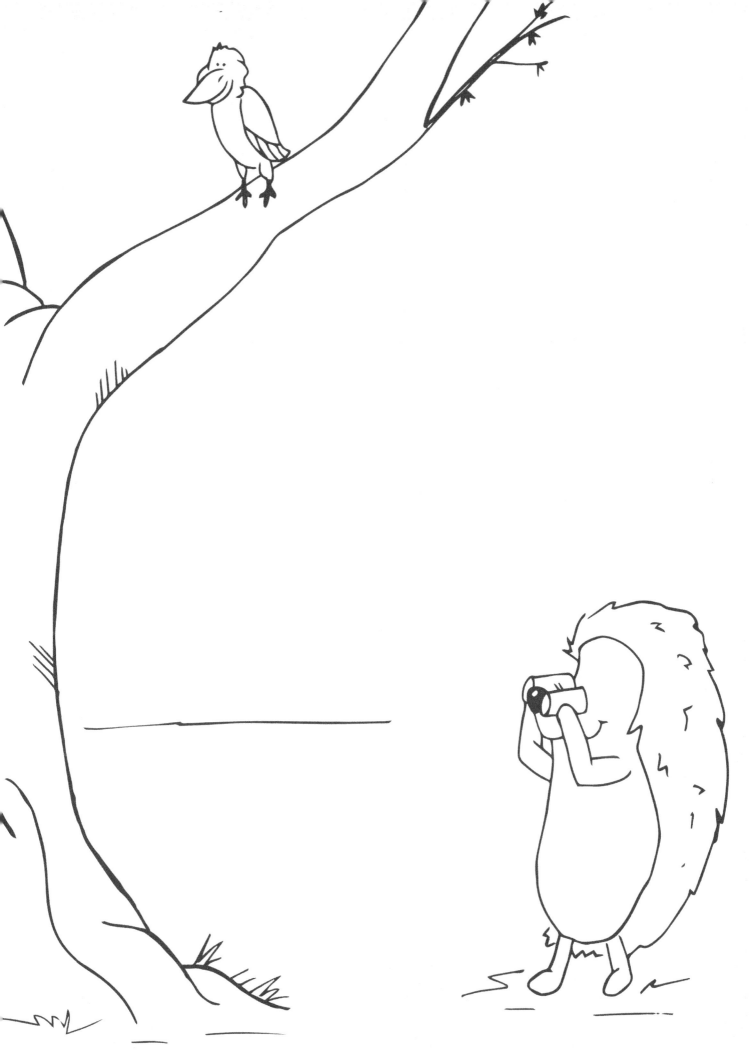

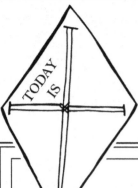

The LORD gives wisdom.
PROVERBS 2:6

This week's verse is :

I am thankful for :

I am praying for :

What I liked about today :

What was hard about today :

How can I show love today?

Today I feel :

What does God say about how I feel?

WELCOME SPRING

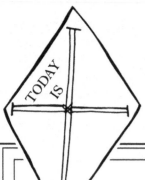

TODAY IS

The LORD gives wisdom.
PROVERBS 2:6

This week's verse is :

I am thankful for :

I am praying for :

What I liked about today :

What was hard about today :

How can I show love today?

Today I feel :

What does God say about how I feel?

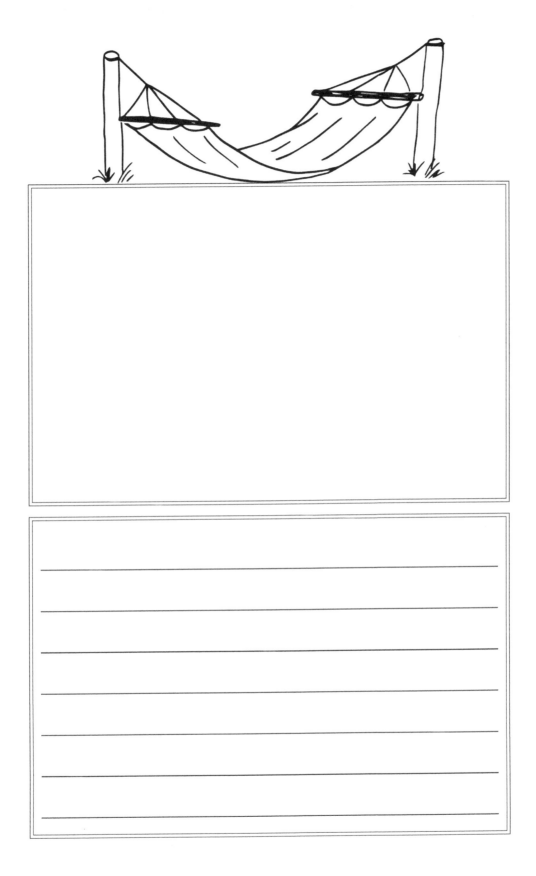

TODAY IS

The LORD gives wisdom.
PROVERBS 2:6

This week's verse is :

I am thankful for :

I am praying for :

What I liked about today :

What was hard about today :

How can I show love today?

Today I feel :

What does God say about how I feel?

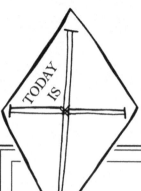

The LORD gives wisdom.
PROVERBS 2:6

This week's verse is :

I am thankful for :

I am praying for :

What I liked about today :

What was hard about today :

How can I show love today?

Today I feel :

What does God say about how I feel?

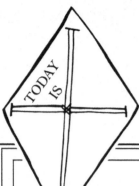

TODAY IS

The LORD gives wisdom.
PROVERBS 2:6

This week's verse is :

I am thankful for :

I am praying for :

What I liked about today :

What was hard about today :

How can I show love today?

Today I feel :

What does God say about how I feel?

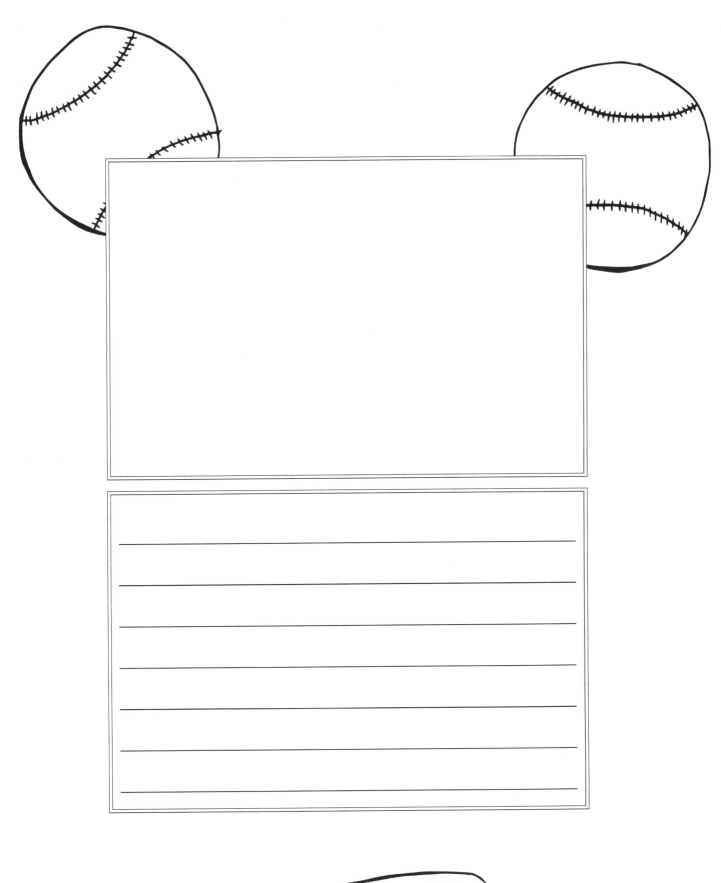

What did this week's verse mean to you?

_____

_____

_____

_____

_____

_____

_____

What was one of your favorite moments this week?

_____

_____

_____

_____

_____

_____

_____

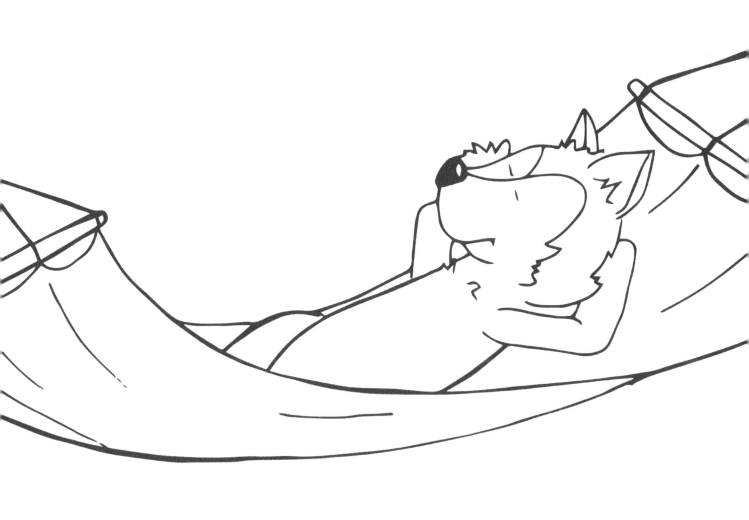

Jesus answered, "I am the way and the truth and the life.
No one comes to the Father except through Me.
JOHN 14:6

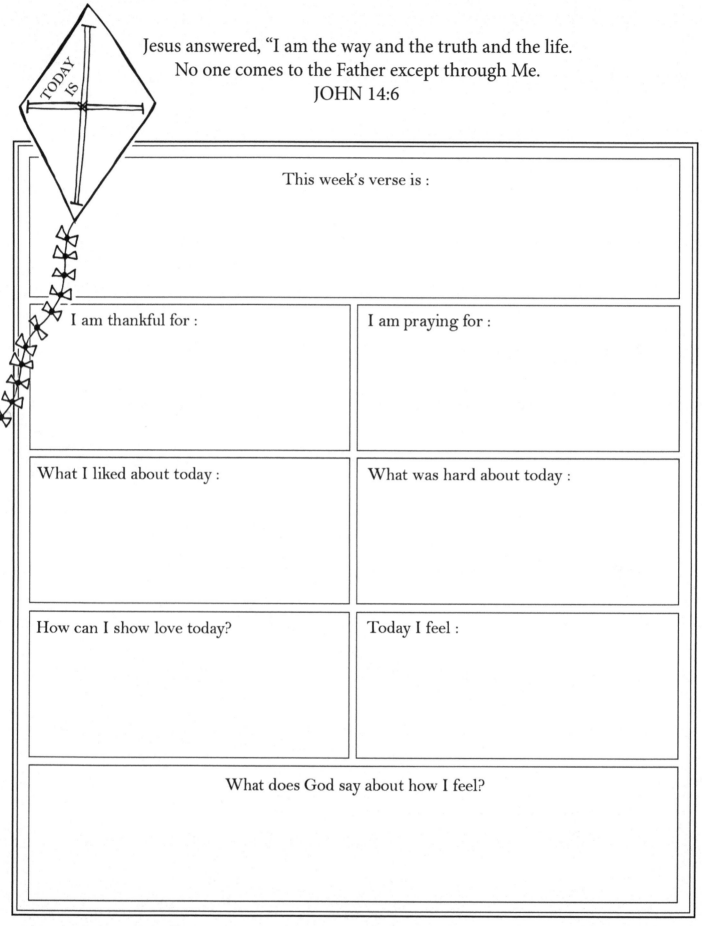

TODAY IS

This week's verse is :

I am thankful for :

I am praying for :

What I liked about today :

What was hard about today :

How can I show love today?

Today I feel :

What does God say about how I feel?

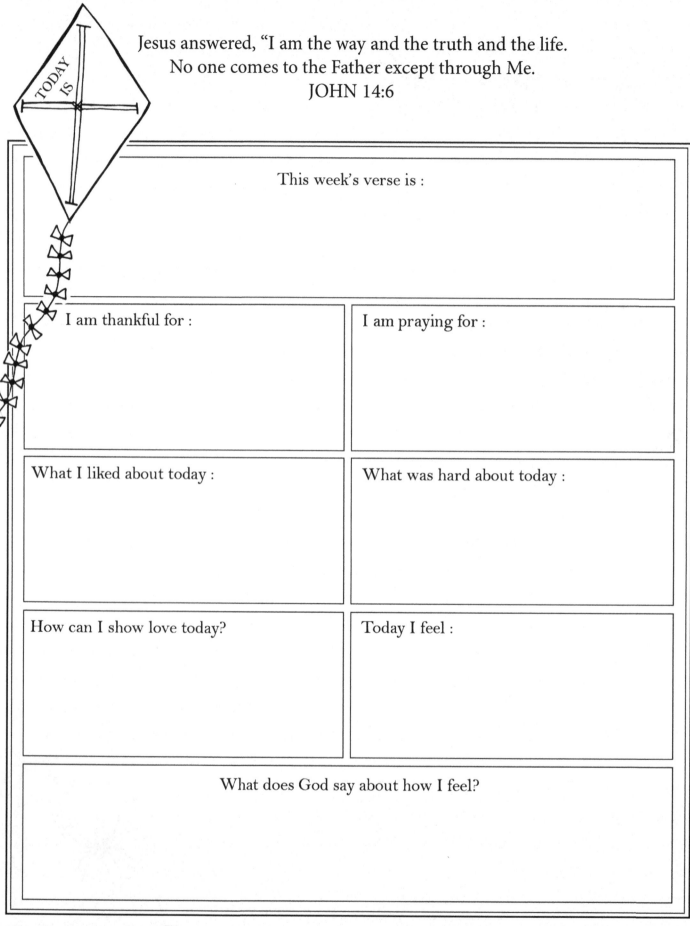

Jesus answered, "I am the way and the truth and the life.
No one comes to the Father except through Me.
JOHN 14:6

TODAY IS

This week's verse is :

I am thankful for :

I am praying for :

What I liked about today :

What was hard about today :

How can I show love today?

Today I feel :

What does God say about how I feel?

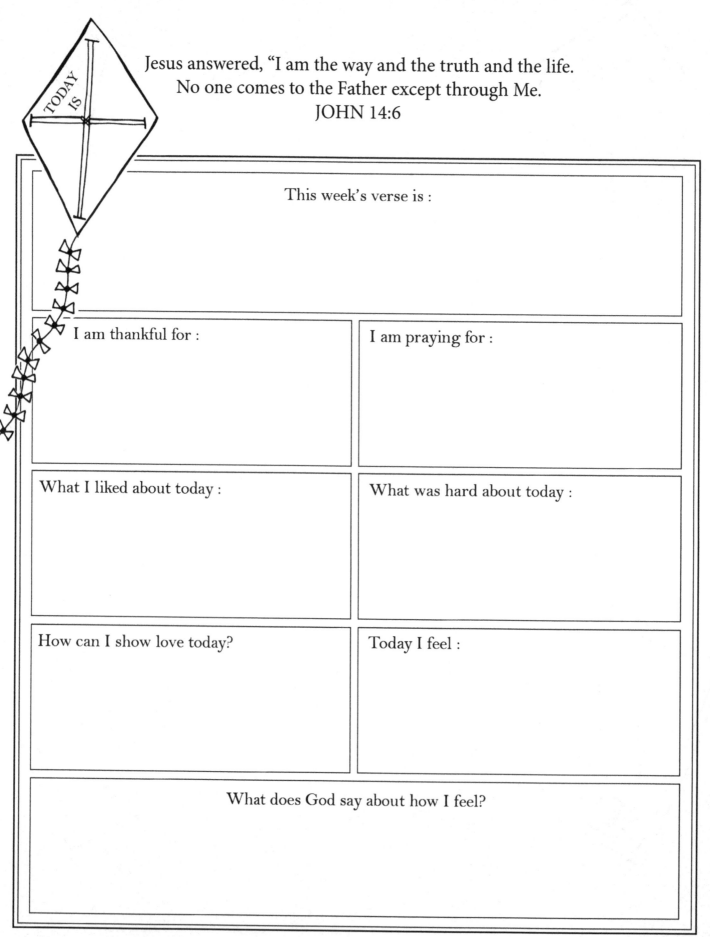

Jesus answered, "I am the way and the truth and the life.
No one comes to the Father except through Me.
JOHN 14:6

TODAY IS

This week's verse is :

I am thankful for :

I am praying for :

What I liked about today :

What was hard about today :

How can I show love today?

Today I feel :

What does God say about how I feel?

Jesus answered, "I am the way and the truth and the life.
No one comes to the Father except through Me.
JOHN 14:6

TODAY IS

This week's verse is :

I am thankful for :

I am praying for :

What I liked about today :

What was hard about today :

How can I show love today?

Today I feel :

What does God say about how I feel?

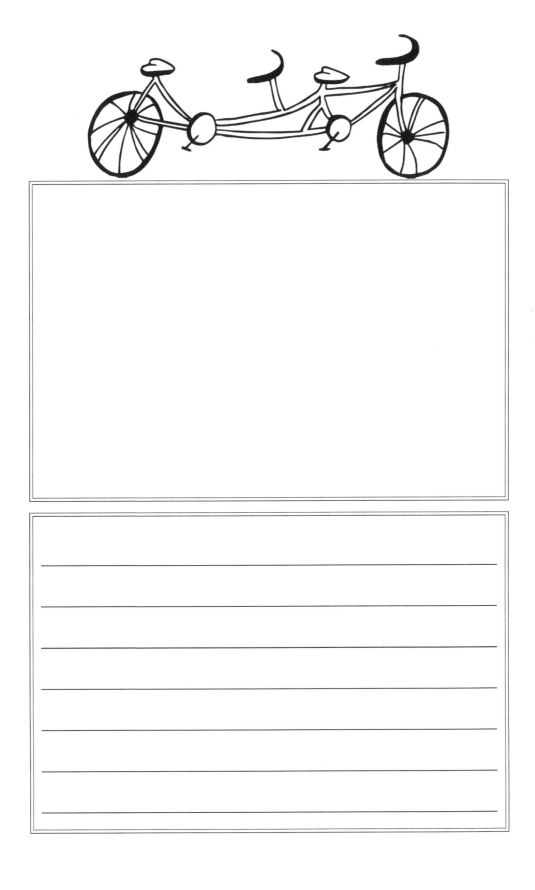

Jesus answered, "I am the way and the truth and the life.
No one comes to the Father except through Me.
JOHN 14:6

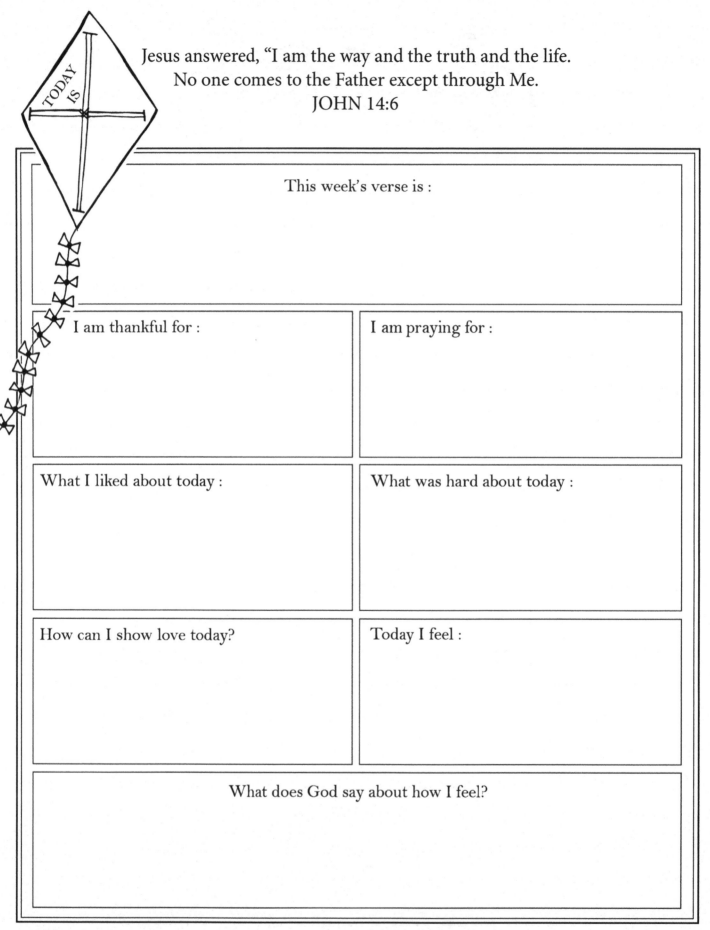

This week's verse is :

I am thankful for :

I am praying for :

What I liked about today :

What was hard about today :

How can I show love today?

Today I feel :

What does God say about how I feel?

#ArchersAdventureJournal

What did this week's verse mean to you?

_____

_____

_____

_____

_____

_____

What was one of your favorite moments this week?

_____

_____

_____

_____

_____

_____

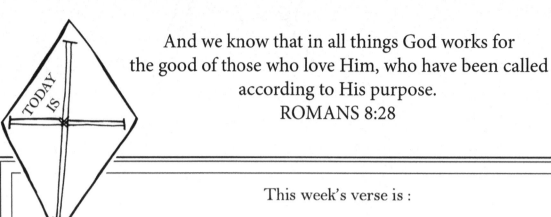

And we know that in all things God works for
the good of those who love Him, who have been called
according to His purpose.
ROMANS 8:28

This week's verse is :

I am thankful for :

I am praying for :

What I liked about today :

What was hard about today :

How can I show love today?

Today I feel :

What does God say about how I feel?

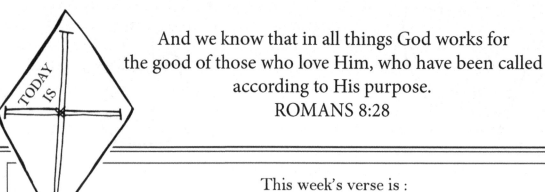

And we know that in all things God works for
the good of those who love Him, who have been called
according to His purpose.
ROMANS 8:28

This week's verse is :

I am thankful for :

I am praying for :

What I liked about today :

What was hard about today :

How can I show love today?

Today I feel :

What does God say about how I feel?

#ArchersAdventureJournal

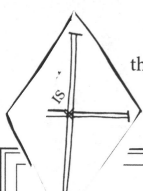

And we know that in all things God works for
the good of those who love Him, who have been called
according to His purpose.
ROMANS 8:28

This week's verse is :

am thankful for :

I am praying for :

What I liked about today :

What was hard about today :

How can I show love today?

Today I feel :

What does God say about how I feel?

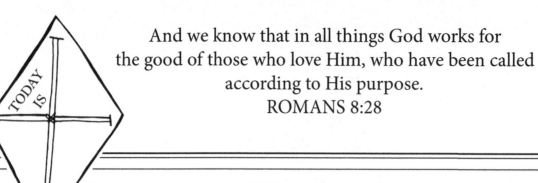

And we know that in all things God works for
the good of those who love Him, who have been called
according to His purpose.
ROMANS 8:28

This week's verse is :

I am thankful for :

I am praying for :

What I liked about today :

What was hard about today :

How can I show love today?

Today I feel :

What does God say about how I feel?

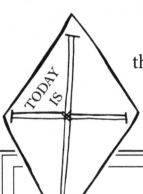

And we know that in all things God works for
the good of those who love Him, who have been called
according to His purpose.
ROMANS 8:28

This week's verse is :

I am thankful for :

I am praying for :

What I liked about today :

What was hard about today :

How can I show love today?

Today I feel :

What does God say about how I feel?

What did this week's verse mean to you?

_____

_____

_____

_____

_____

_____

_____

What was one of your favorite moments this week?

_____

_____

_____

_____

_____

_____

_____

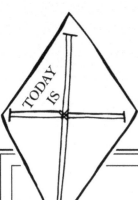

But He said to me, "My grace is sufficient for you,
for My power is made perfect in weakness."
2 CORINTHIANS 12:9

This week's verse is :

I am thankful for :

I am praying for :

What I liked about today :

What was hard about today :

How can I show love today?

Today I feel :

What does God say about how I feel?

#ArchersAdventureJournal

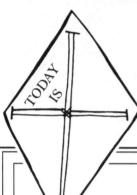

But He said to me, "My grace is sufficient for you,
for My power is made perfect in weakness."
2 CORINTHIANS 12:9

This week's verse is :

I am thankful for :

I am praying for :

What I liked about today :

What was hard about today :

How can I show love today?

Today I feel :

What does God say about how I feel?

#ArchersAdventureJournal

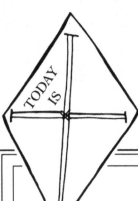
TODAY IS

But He said to me, "My grace is sufficient for you,
for My power is made perfect in weakness."
2 CORINTHIANS 12:9

This week's verse is :

I am thankful for :

I am praying for :

What I liked about today :

What was hard about today :

How can I show love today?

Today I feel :

What does God say about how I feel?

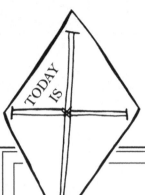

But He said to me, "My grace is sufficient for you, for My power is made perfect in weakness."
2 CORINTHIANS 12:9

This week's verse is :

I am thankful for :

I am praying for :

What I liked about today :

What was hard about today :

How can I show love today?

Today I feel :

What does God say about how I feel?

#ArchersAdventureJournal

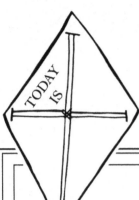

But He said to me, "My grace is sufficient for you,
for My power is made perfect in weakness."
2 CORINTHIANS 12:9

This week's verse is :

I am thankful for :

I am praying for :

What I liked about today :

What was hard about today :

How can I show love today?

Today I feel :

What does God say about how I feel?

#ArchersAdventureJournal

What did this week's verse mean to you?

_____

_____

_____

_____

_____

_____

_____

What was one of your favorite moments this week?

_____

_____

_____

_____

_____

_____

_____

Submit yourselves, then, to God.
Resist the devil, and he will flee from you.
JAMES 4:7

This week's verse is :

I am thankful for :

I am praying for :

What I liked about today :

What was hard about today :

How can I show love today?

Today I feel :

What does God say about how I feel?

WELCOME SPRING

#ArchersAdventureJournal

Submit yourselves, then, to God.
Resist the devil, and he will flee from you.
JAMES 4:7

This week's verse is :

I am thankful for :

I am praying for :

What I liked about today :

What was hard about today :

How can I show love today?

Today I feel :

What does God say about how I feel?

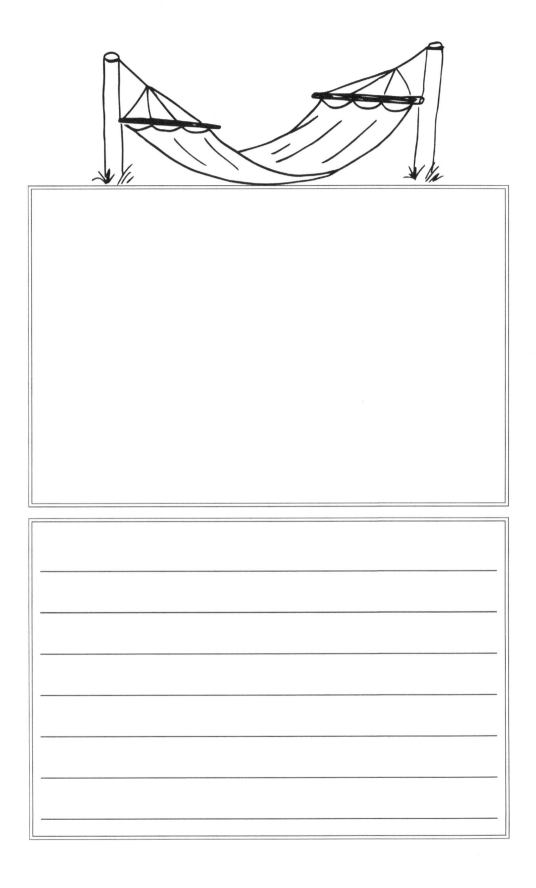

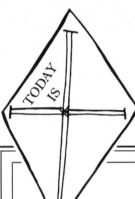

Submit yourselves, then, to God.
Resist the devil, and he will flee from you.
JAMES 4:7

This week's verse is :

I am thankful for :

I am praying for :

What I liked about today :

What was hard about today :

How can I show love today?

Today I feel :

What does God say about how I feel?

Submit yourselves, then, to God.
Resist the devil, and he will flee from you.
JAMES 4:7

This week's verse is :

I am thankful for :

I am praying for :

What I liked about today :

What was hard about today :

How can I show love today?

Today I feel :

What does God say about how I feel?

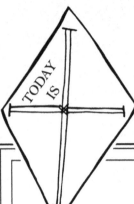

Submit yourselves, then, to God.
Resist the devil, and he will flee from you.
JAMES 4:7

This week's verse is :

I am thankful for :

I am praying for :

What I liked about today :

What was hard about today :

How can I show love today?

Today I feel :

What does God say about how I feel?

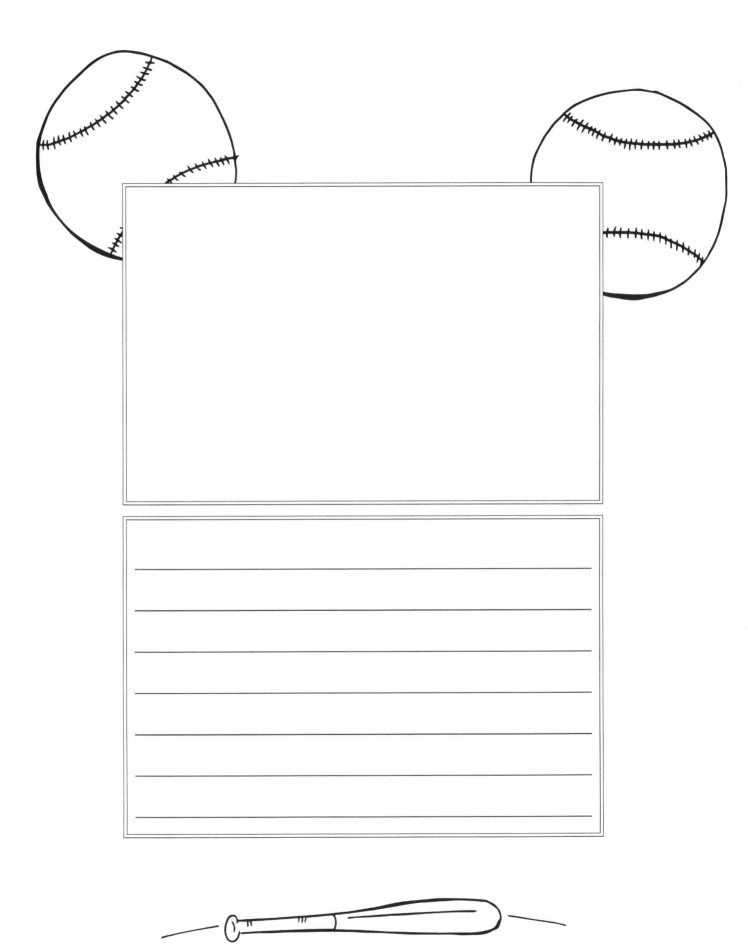

#ArchersAdventureJournal

What did this week's verse mean to you?

_____

_____

_____

_____

_____

_____

_____

What was one of your favorite moments this week?

_____

_____

_____

_____

_____

_____

_____

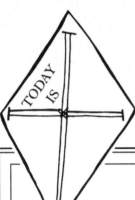

TODAY IS

Do not merely listen to the word, and so deceive yourselves. Do what it says.
JAMES 1:22

This week's verse is :

I am thankful for :

I am praying for :

What I liked about today :

What was hard about today :

How can I show love today?

Today I feel :

What does God say about how I feel?

#ArchersAdventureJournal

Do not merely listen to the word, and so
deceive yourselves. Do what it says.
JAMES 1:22

TODAY IS

This week's verse is :

I am thankful for :

I am praying for :

What I liked about today :

What was hard about today :

How can I show love today?

Today I feel :

What does God say about how I feel?

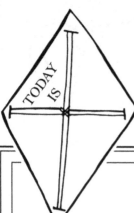

Do not merely listen to the word, and so
deceive yourselves. Do what it says.
JAMES 1:22

This week's verse is :

I am thankful for :

I am praying for :

What I liked about today :

What was hard about today :

How can I show love today?

Today I feel :

What does God say about how I feel?

#ArchersAdventureJournal

Do not merely listen to the word, and so
deceive yourselves. Do what it says.
JAMES 1:22

This week's verse is :

I am thankful for :

I am praying for :

What I liked about today :

What was hard about today :

How can I show love today?

Today I feel :

What does God say about how I feel?

TODAY IS

Do not merely listen to the word, and so deceive yourselves. Do what it says.
JAMES 1:22

This week's verse is :

I am thankful for :

I am praying for :

What I liked about today :

What was hard about today :

How can I show love today?

Today I feel :

What does God say about how I feel?

#ArchersAdventureJournal

What did this week's verse mean to you?

_____

_____

_____

_____

_____

_____

_____

What was one of your favorite moments this week?

_____

_____

_____

_____

_____

_____

_____

But the fruit of the Spirit is love, joy, peace, patience, kindness, goodness, faithfulness, gentleness and self-control.
GALATIANS 5:22

TODAY IS

This week's verse is :

I am thankful for :

I am praying for :

What I liked about today :

What was hard about today :

How can I show love today?

Today I feel :

What does God say about how I feel?

But the fruit of the Spirit is love, joy, peace, patience, kindness, goodness, faithfulness, gentleness and self-control.
GALATIANS 5:22

TODAY IS

This week's verse is :

I am thankful for :

I am praying for :

What I liked about today :

What was hard about today :

How can I show love today?

Today I feel :

What does God say about how I feel?

#ArchersAdventureJournal

But the fruit of the Spirit is love, joy, peace, patience, kindness, goodness, faithfulness, gentleness and self-control.
GALATIANS 5:22

TODAY IS

This week's verse is :

I am thankful for :

I am praying for :

What I liked about today :

What was hard about today :

How can I show love today?

Today I feel :

What does God say about how I feel?

But the fruit of the Spirit is love, joy, peace, patience, kindness, goodness, faithfulness, gentleness and self-control.
GALATIANS 5:22

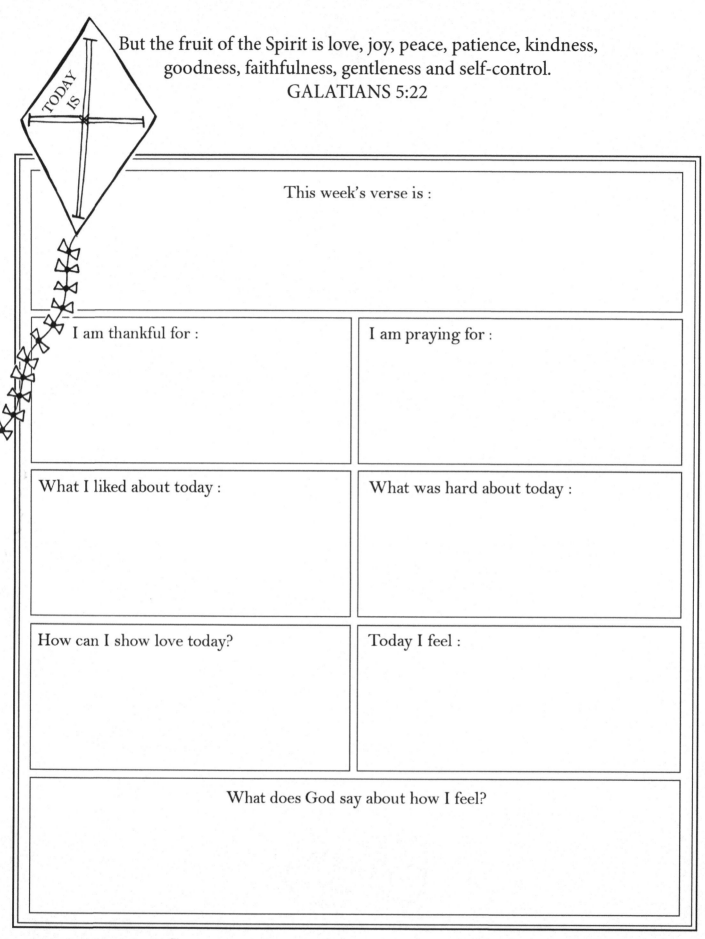

TODAY IS

This week's verse is :

I am thankful for :

I am praying for :

What I liked about today :

What was hard about today :

How can I show love today?

Today I feel :

What does God say about how I feel?

But the fruit of the Spirit is love, joy, peace, patience, kindness, goodness, faithfulness, gentleness and self-control.
GALATIANS 5:22

TODAY IS

This week's verse is :

I am thankful for :

I am praying for :

What I liked about today :

What was hard about today :

How can I show love today?

Today I feel :

What does God say about how I feel?

What did this week's verse mean to you?

_____

_____

_____

_____

_____

_____

_____

What was one of your favorite moments this week?

_____

_____

_____

_____

_____

_____

_____

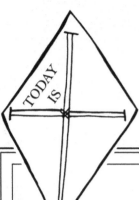

Give thanks in all circumstances,
for this is God's will for you in Christ Jesus.
1 THESSALONIANS 5:18

This week's verse is :

I am thankful for :

I am praying for :

What I liked about today :

What was hard about today :

How can I show love today?

Today I feel :

What does God say about how I feel?

#ArchersAdventureJournal

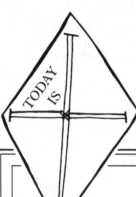

Give thanks in all circumstances,
for this is God's will for you in Christ Jesus.
1 THESSALONIANS 5:18

This week's verse is :

I am thankful for :

I am praying for :

What I liked about today :

What was hard about today :

How can I show love today?

Today I feel :

What does God say about how I feel?

Give thanks in all circumstances,
for this is God's will for you in Christ Jesus.
1 THESSALONIANS 5:18

This week's verse is :

I am thankful for :

I am praying for :

What I liked about today :

What was hard about today :

How can I show love today?

Today I feel :

What does God say about how I feel?

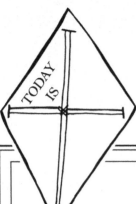

Give thanks in all circumstances,
for this is God's will for you in Christ Jesus.
1 THESSALONIANS 5:18

This week's verse is :

I am thankful for :

I am praying for :

What I liked about today :

What was hard about today :

How can I show love today?

Today I feel :

What does God say about how I feel?

#ArchersAdventureJournal

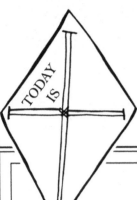

Give thanks in all circumstances,
for this is God's will for you in Christ Jesus.
1 THESSALONIANS 5:18

This week's verse is :

I am thankful for :

I am praying for :

What I liked about today :

What was hard about today :

How can I show love today?

Today I feel :

What does God say about how I feel?

What did this week's verse mean to you?

_____

_____

_____

_____

_____

_____

_____

What was one of your favorite moments this week?

_____

_____

_____

_____

_____

_____

_____

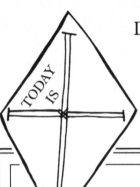

Do not be anxious about anything, but in everything, by prayer and petition, with thanksgiving, present your requests to God.
PHILIPPIANS 4:6

This week's verse is :

I am thankful for :

I am praying for :

What I liked about today :

What was hard about today :

How can I show love today?

Today I feel :

What does God say about how I feel?

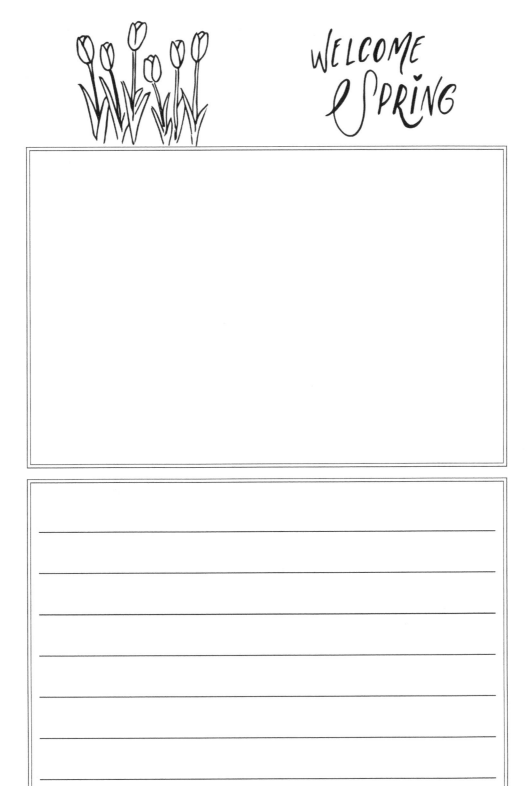

WELCOME SPRING

Do not be anxious about anything, but in everything,
by prayer and petition, with thanksgiving,
present your requests to God.
PHILIPPIANS 4:6

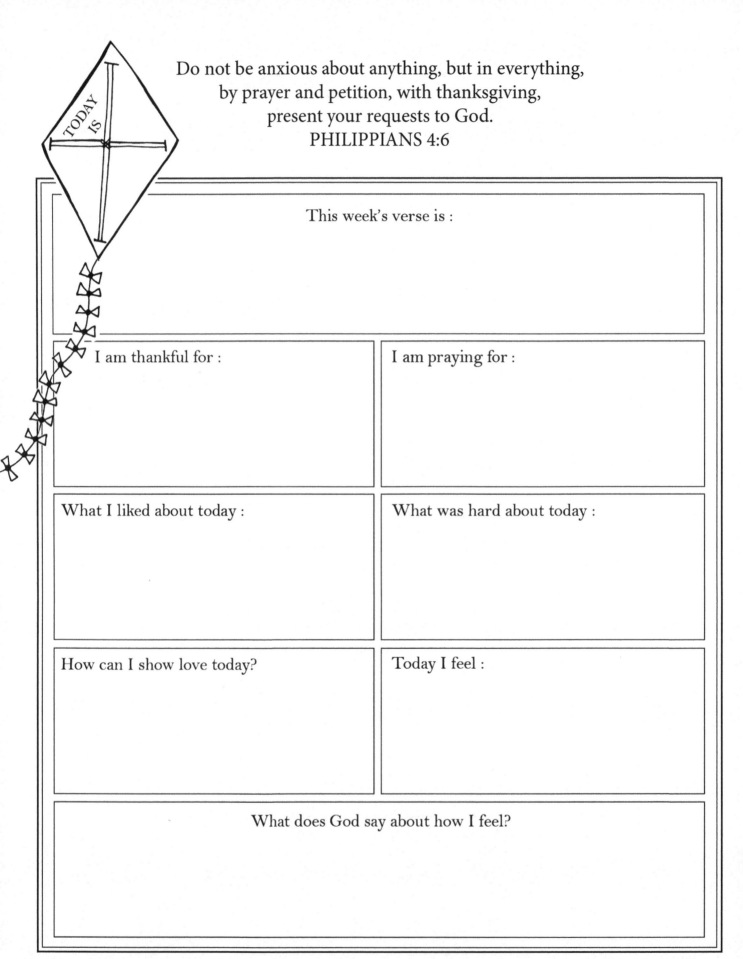

TODAY IS

This week's verse is :

I am thankful for :

I am praying for :

What I liked about today :

What was hard about today :

How can I show love today?

Today I feel :

What does God say about how I feel?

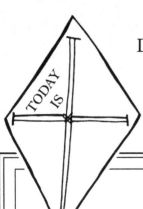

Do not be anxious about anything, but in everything,
by prayer and petition, with thanksgiving,
present your requests to God.
PHILIPPIANS 4:6

This week's verse is :

I am thankful for :

I am praying for :

What I liked about today :

What was hard about today :

How can I show love today?

Today I feel :

What does God say about how I feel?

Do not be anxious about anything, but in everything,
by prayer and petition, with thanksgiving,
present your requests to God.
PHILIPPIANS 4:6

TODAY IS

This week's verse is :

I am thankful for :

I am praying for :

What I liked about today :

What was hard about today :

How can I show love today?

Today I feel :

What does God say about how I feel?

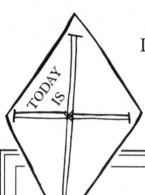

TODAY IS

Do not be anxious about anything, but in everything,
by prayer and petition, with thanksgiving,
present your requests to God.
PHILIPPIANS 4:6

This week's verse is :

I am thankful for :

I am praying for :

What I liked about today :

What was hard about today :

How can I show love today?

Today I feel :

What does God say about how I feel?

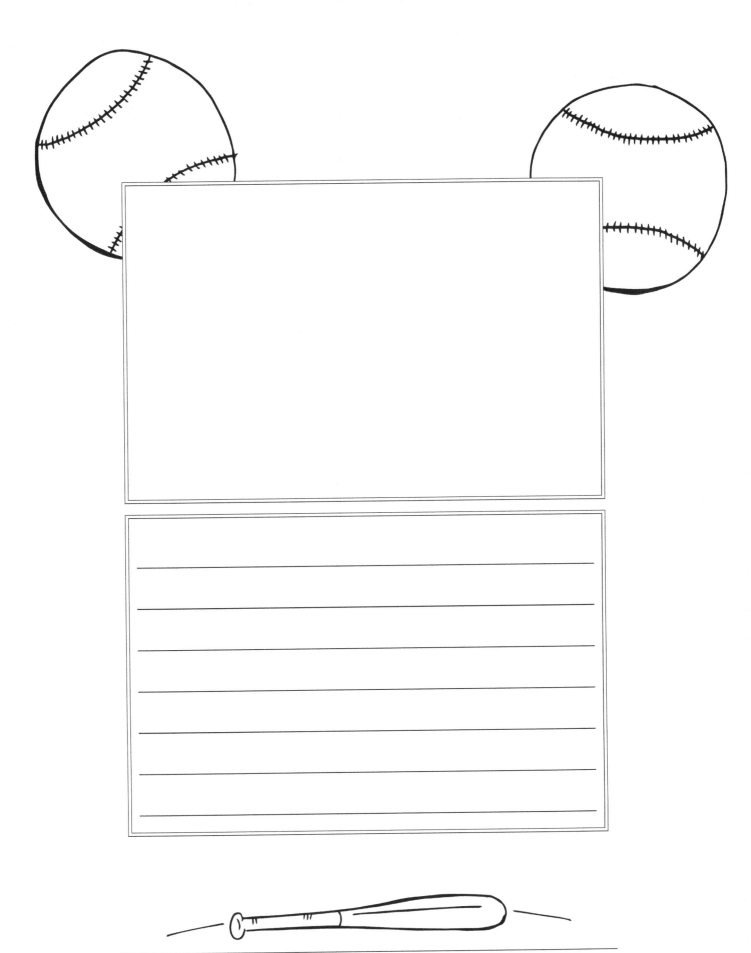

What did this week's verse mean to you?

_____

_____

_____

_____

_____

_____

_____

What was one of your favorite moments this week?

_____

_____

_____

_____

_____

_____

_____

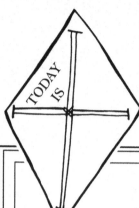

And the peace of God, which transcends all understanding, will guard your hearts and your minds in Christ Jesus.
PHILIPPIANS 4:7

This week's verse is :

I am thankful for :

I am praying for :

What I liked about today :

What was hard about today :

How can I show love today?

Today I feel :

What does God say about how I feel?

#ArchersAdventureJournal

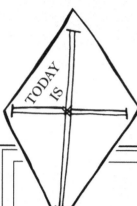

TODAY IS

And the peace of God, which transcends all understanding, will guard your hearts and your minds in Christ Jesus.
PHILIPPIANS 4:7

This week's verse is :

I am thankful for :

I am praying for :

What I liked about today :

What was hard about today :

How can I show love today?

Today I feel :

What does God say about how I feel?

And the peace of God, which transcends all understanding, will guard your hearts and your minds in Christ Jesus.
PHILIPPIANS 4:7

This week's verse is :

I am thankful for :

I am praying for :

What I liked about today :

What was hard about today :

How can I show love today?

Today I feel :

What does God say about how I feel?

#ArchersAdventureJournal

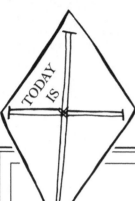

And the peace of God, which transcends all understanding, will guard your hearts and your minds in Christ Jesus.
PHILIPPIANS 4:7

This week's verse is :

I am thankful for :

I am praying for :

What I liked about today :

What was hard about today :

How can I show love today?

Today I feel :

What does God say about how I feel?

And the peace of God, which transcends all
understanding, will guard your hearts and
your minds in Christ Jesus.
PHILIPPIANS 4:7

This week's verse is :

I am thankful for :

I am praying for :

What I liked about today :

What was hard about today :

How can I show love today?

Today I feel :

What does God say about how I feel?

What did this week's verse mean to you?

_____

_____

_____

_____

_____

_____

_____

What was one of your favorite moments this week?

_____

_____

_____

_____

_____

_____

_____

All Scripture is God-breathed and is useful for teaching, rebuking, correcting, and training in righteousness.
2 TIMOTHY 3:16

TODAY IS

This week's verse is :

I am thankful for :

I am praying for :

What I liked about today :

What was hard about today :

How can I show love today?

Today I feel :

What does God say about how I feel?

All Scripture is God-breathed and is useful for teaching, rebuking, correcting, and training in righteousness.
2 TIMOTHY 3:16

TODAY IS

This week's verse is :

I am thankful for :

I am praying for :

What I liked about today :

What was hard about today :

How can I show love today?

Today I feel :

What does God say about how I feel?

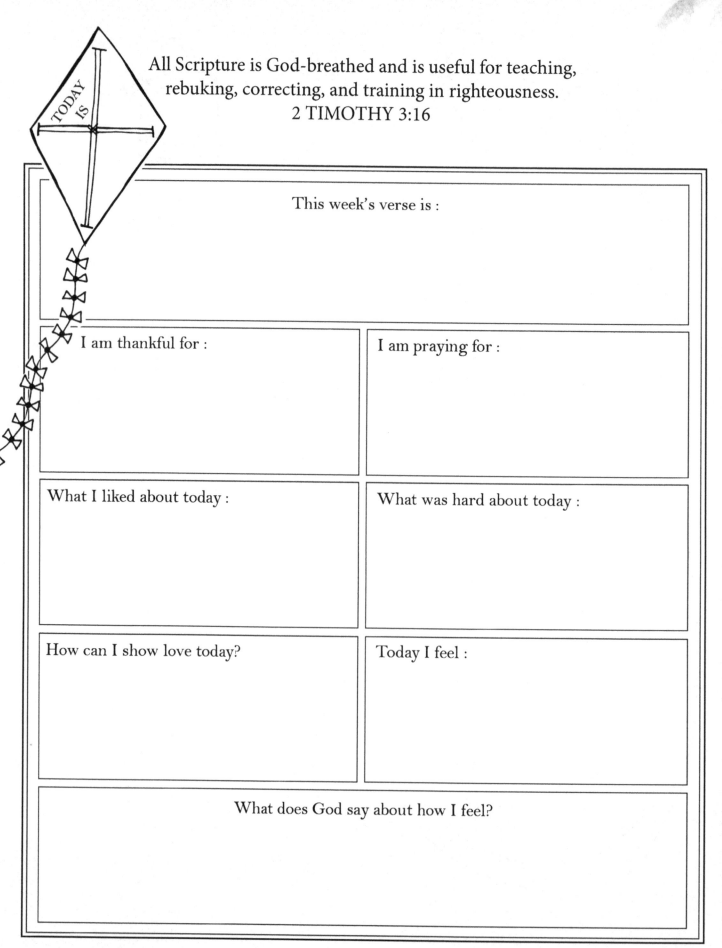

All Scripture is God-breathed and is useful for teaching, rebuking, correcting, and training in righteousness.
2 TIMOTHY 3:16

TODAY IS

This week's verse is :

I am thankful for :

I am praying for :

What I liked about today :

What was hard about today :

How can I show love today?

Today I feel :

What does God say about how I feel?

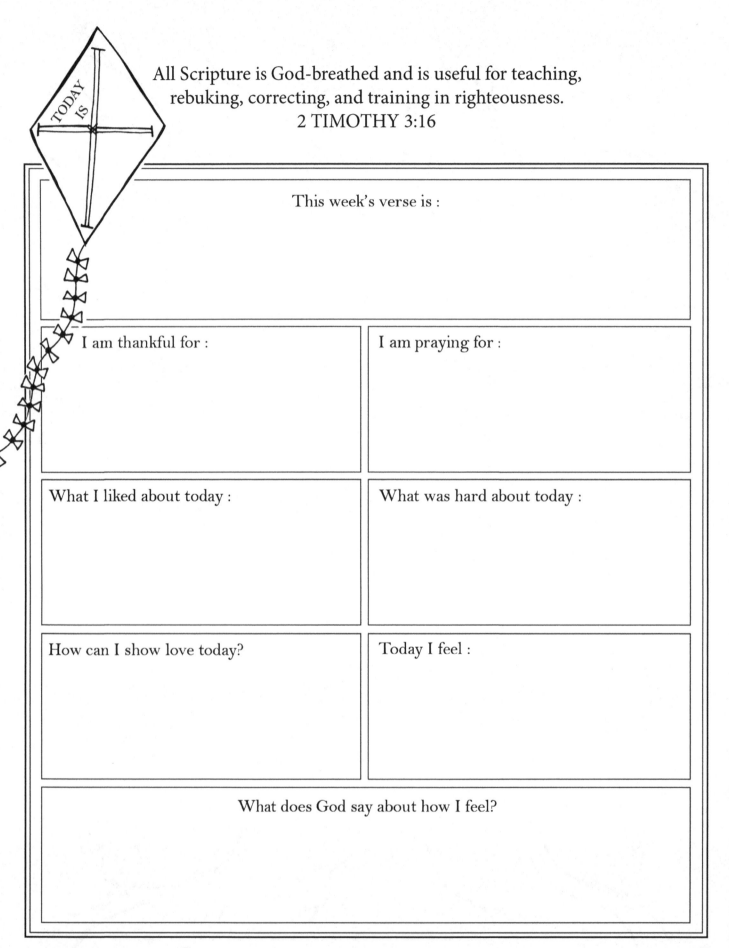

All Scripture is God-breathed and is useful for teaching, rebuking, correcting, and training in righteousness.
2 TIMOTHY 3:16

TODAY IS

This week's verse is :

I am thankful for :

I am praying for :

What I liked about today :

What was hard about today :

How can I show love today?

Today I feel :

What does God say about how I feel?

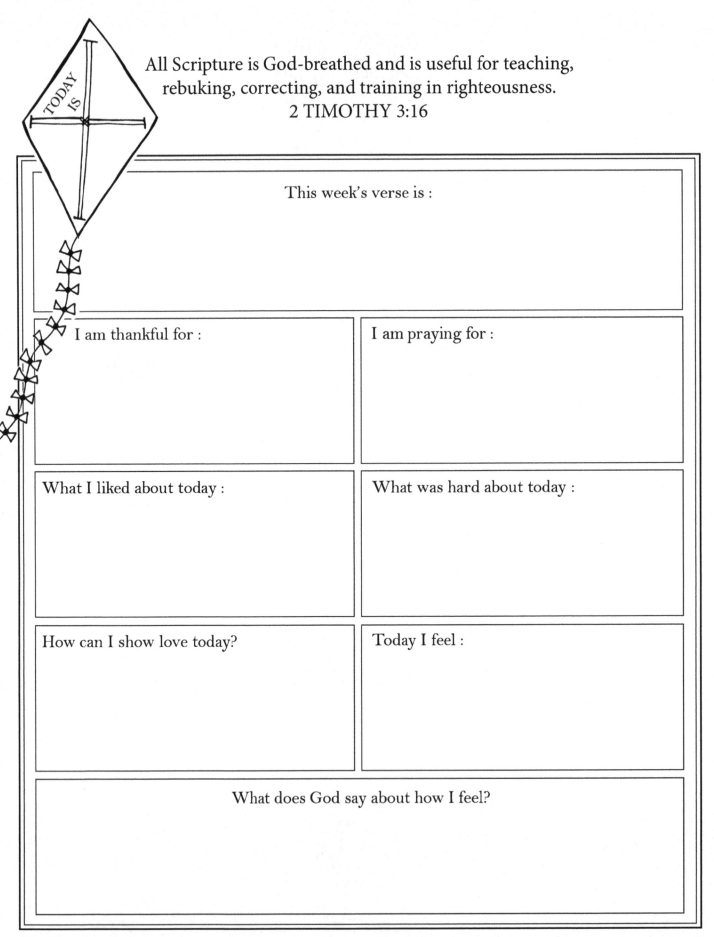

All Scripture is God-breathed and is useful for teaching, rebuking, correcting, and training in righteousness.
2 TIMOTHY 3:16

TODAY IS

This week's verse is :

I am thankful for :

I am praying for :

What I liked about today :

What was hard about today :

How can I show love today?

Today I feel :

What does God say about how I feel?

What did this week's verse mean to you?

_____

_____

_____

_____

_____

_____

_____

What was one of your favorite moments this week?

_____

_____

_____

_____

_____

_____

_____

Bible Verses Feelings Guide

You can find out what God has to say about how you feel in the following pages.

Use this guide to explore God's Word, and help you fill out your daily pages.

Afraid

Psalm 23:4 - Even when I walk through the darkest valley, I will not be afraid, for you are close beside me. Your rod and your staff protect and comfort me. NLT

Isaiah 41:13 - For I am the LORD your God who takes hold of your right hand and says to you, Do not fear; I will help you. NIV

Psalm 27:1 - The LORD is my light and my salvation; whom shall I fear? The LORD is the stronghold of my life; of whom shall I be afraid? ESV

Alone

Matthew 28:20 - Teach these new disciples to obey all the commands I have given you. And be sure of this: I am with you always, even to the end of the age. NLT

Romans 8:38 - And I am convinced that nothing can ever separate us from God's love. Neither death nor life, neither angels nor demons, neither our fears for today nor our worries about tomorrow-not even the powers of hell can separate us from God's love. NLT

Angry

Ephesians 4:26-27 - And "don't sin by letting anger control you." Don't let the sun go down while you are still angry, for anger gives a foothold to the devil. NLT

Annoyed

Colossians 3:13 - Bear with each other and forgive one another if any of you has a grievance against someone. Forgive as the Lord forgave you. NIV

Anxious

Philippians 4:6 - Don't worry about anything; instead, pray about everything. Tell God what you need, and thank him for all he has done. NLT

Bold

Proverbs 28:1 - The wicked flee though no one pursues, but the righteous are as bold as a lion. NIV

Bossy

Romans 12:16 - Live in harmony with each other. Don't be too proud to enjoy the company of ordinary people. And don't think you know it all! NLT

1 Corinthians 13:4-6 - Love is patient and kind; love does not envy or boast; it is not arrogant or rude. It does not insist on its own way; it is not irritable or resentful; it does not rejoice at wrongdoing, but rejoices with the truth. ESV

Brave

Hebrews 13:6 - So we can confidently say, "The Lord is my helper; I will not fear; what can man do to me?" ESV

Psalm 31:24 - So be strong and courageous, all you who put your hope in the LORD! NLT

Calm

Psalm 23:1-3 - The LORD is my shepherd, I lack nothing. He makes me lie down in green pastures, he leads me beside quiet waters, he refreshes my soul. He guides me along the right paths. NIV

Conceited

Isaiah 5:21 - What sorrow for those who are wise in their own eyes and think themselves so clever. NLT

Proverbs 28:26 - Those who trust in themselves are fools, but those who walk in wisdom are kept safe. NIV

Confident

Proverbs 14:26 - In the fear of the LORD one has strong confidence, and his children will have a refuge. ESV

Confused

1 Corinthians 14:33 - For God is not a God of confusion but of peace. (shortened) ESV

Courageous

Joshua 1:9 - This is my command-be strong and courageous! Do not be afraid or discouraged. For the LORD your God is with you wherever you go." NLT

Different

Genesis 1:27 - So God created mankind in his own image, in the image of God he created them; male and female he created them. NIV

1 Peter 2:9 - But you are a chosen people, a royal priesthood, a holy nation, God's special possession, that you may declare the praises of him who called you out of darkness into his wonderful light. NIV

Disappointed

Deuteronomy 31:8 - Do not be afraid or discouraged, for the LORD will personally go ahead of you. He will be with you; he will neither fail you nor abandon you." NLT

John 14:27 - "I am leaving you with a gift-peace of mind and heart. And the peace I give is a gift the world cannot give. So don't be troubled or afraid. NLT

Doubtful

Proverbs 3:5-6 - Trust in the LORD with all your heart; do not depend on your own understanding. Seek his will in all you do, and he will show you which path to take. NLT

Embarrassed

2 Timothy 2:15 - Do your best to present yourself to God as one approved, a worker who does not need to be ashamed and who correctly handles the word of truth. NIV

Empty

John 10:10 - The thief comes only to steal and kill and destroy; I have come that they may have life, and have it to the full. NIV

Excited

Isaiah 55:12 - You will go out in joy and be led forth in peace; the mountains and hills will burst into song before you, and all the trees of the field will clap their hands. NIV

Explosive

Ephesians 4:31 - Get rid of all bitterness, rage, anger, harsh words, and slander, as well as all types of evil behavior. NLT

Proverbs 29:11 - Fools vent their anger, but the wise quietly hold it back. NLT

James 1:20 - Human anger does not produce the righteousness God desires. NLT

Frustrated

Psalm 46:10 - "Be still, and know that I am God. I will be exalted among the nations, I will be exalted in the earth!" ESV

Grouchy

Philippians 2:14 - Do everything without complaining and arguing. NLT

Guilty

Colossians 1:13-14 - He has delivered us from the domain of darkness and transferred us to the kingdom of his beloved Son, in whom we have redemption, the forgiveness of sins. ESV

Happy

Psalm 144:15 - Yes, joyful are those who live like this! Joyful indeed are those whose God is the LORD. NLT

Heartbroken

Psalm 34:18 - The LORD is close to the brokenhearted; he rescues those whose spirits are crushed. NLT

Helpless

Psalm 46:1 - God is our refuge and strength, a very present help in trouble. ESV

Psalm 28:7-8 - The LORD is my strength and shield. I trust him with all my heart. He helps me, and my heart is filled with joy. I burst out in songs of thanksgiving. The LORD gives his people strength. He is a safe fortress for his anointed king. NLT

Hopeless

Hebrews 4:16 - So let us come boldly to the throne of our gracious God. There we will receive his mercy, and we will find grace to help us when we need it most. NLT

Hopeful

Romans 5:5 - And this hope will not lead to disappointment. For we know how dearly God loves us, because he has given us the Holy Spirit to fill our hearts with his love. NLT

Hurt

Psalm 147:3 - He heals the brokenhearted and binds up their wounds. NIV

Psalm 30:5 - For his anger lasts only a moment, but his favor lasts a lifetime! Weeping may last through the night, but joy comes with the morning. NLT

Psalm 146:8 - The LORD opens the eyes of the blind. The LORD lifts up those who are weighed down. The LORD loves the godly. NLT

Impatient

Proverbs 14:29 - Whoever is patient has great understanding, but one who is quick-tempered displays folly. NIV

Incapable

2 Corinthians 12:9 - Each time he said, "My grace is all you need. My power works best in weakness." So now I am glad to boast about my weaknesses, so that the power of Christ can work through me. NLT

Joyful

Psalm 32:11 - Rejoice in the LORD and be glad, you righteous; sing, all you who are upright in heart! NIV

Kind

Ephesians 4:32 - Instead, be kind to each other, tenderhearted, forgiving one another, just as God through Christ has forgiven you. NLT

Lonely

Zephaniah 3:17 - For the LORD your God is living among you. He is a mighty savior. He will take delight in you with gladness. With his love, he will calm all your fears. He will rejoice over you with joyful songs. NLT

Lost

Isaiah 41:10 - So do not fear, for I am with you; do not be dismayed, for I am your God. I will strengthen you and help you; I will uphold you with my righteous right hand. NIV

Loved

Psalm 86:15 - But you, Lord, are a compassionate and gracious God, slow to anger, abounding in love and faithfulness. NIV

Mad

James 1:19-20 - Know this, my beloved brothers: let every person be quick to hear, slow to speak, slow to anger; for the anger of man does not produce the righteousness of God. ESV

Mean

Ephesians 4:29 - Let no corrupting talk come out of your mouths, but only such as is good for building up, as fits the occasion, that it may give grace to those who hear. ESV

John 13:34 - A new command I give you: Love one another. As I have loved you, so you must love one another. NIV

Nervous

Isaiah 40:30-31 - Even youths will become weak and tired, and young men will fall in exhaustion. But those who trust in the LORD will find new strength. They will soar high on wings like eagles. They will run and not grow weary. They will walk and not faint. NLT

Peaceful

Isaiah 26:3 - You will keep in perfect peace all who trust in you, all whose thoughts are fixed on you! NLT

Proud

James 4:6 - But he gives us even more grace to stand against such evil desires. As the Scriptures say, "God opposes the proud but favors the humble." NLT

Proverbs 29:23 - A man's pride will bring him low, But a humble spirit will obtain honor. NASB

Sad

Psalm 34:17 - When the righteous cry for help, the LORD hears and delivers them out of all their troubles. ESV

Scared

Psalm 55:22 - Cast your burden on the LORD, and he will sustain you; he will never permit the righteous to be moved. ESV

Proverbs 29:25 - Fear of man will prove to be a snare, but whoever trusts in the LORD is kept safe. NIV

John 14:27 - I am leaving you with a gift--peace of mind and heart. And the peace I give is a gift the world cannot give. So don't be troubled or afraid. NLT

Psalm 56:3 - When I am afraid, I put my trust in you. NIV

Selfish

James 3:16 - For where you have envy and selfish ambition, there you find disorder and every evil practice. NIV

Philippians 2:3 - Don't be selfish; don't try to impress others. Be humble, thinking of others as better than yourselves. NLT

Shy

2 Timothy 1:7 - For the Spirit God gave us does not make us timid, but gives us power, love and self-control. NIV

Shame

2 Corinthians 5:17 - This means that anyone who belongs to Christ has become a new person. The old life is gone; a new life has begun! NLT

Isaiah 53:5 - But he was pierced for our transgressions, he was crushed for our iniquities; the punishment that brought us peace was on him, and by his wounds we are healed. NIV

Sorry

1 John 1:9 - If we confess our sins, he is faithful and just and will forgive us our sins and purify us from all unrighteousness. NIV

Threatened

Psalm 27:5 - For he will conceal me there when troubles come; he will hide me in his sanctuary. He will place me out of reach on a high rock. NLT

2 Samuel 22:3 - My God is my rock, in whom I find protection. He is my shield, the power that saves me, and my place of safety. He is my refuge, my savior, the one who saves me from violence. NLT

Tired

Matthew 11:28 - "Come to me, all you who are weary and burdened, and I will give you rest. NIV

Unloved

John 3:16 - For God loved the world so much that he gave his one and only Son, so that everyone who believes in him will not perish but have eternal life. NLT

Unsure

Matthew 7:7 - "Ask, and it will be given to you; seek, and you will find; knock, and it will be opened to you." ESV

Weak

Isaiah 40:29 - He gives strength to the weary and increases the power of the weak. NIV

Worried

1 Peter 5:7 - Give all your worries and cares to God, for he cares about you. NLT

Worthless

Psalm 139:13-14 - For you created my inmost being; you knit me together in my mother's womb. I praise you because I am fearfully and wonderfully made; your works are wonderful, I know that full well. NIV

Psalm 56:8 - You keep track of all my sorrows. You have collected all my tears in your bottle. You have recorded each one in your book. NLT

1 Corinthians 16:20 - For God bought you with a high price. So you must honor God with your body. NLT

Meet The Author

Karen Stott is a visionary, entrepreneur, and fireman's wife, and author of An Intentional Life, and Intentional Days. She found her heartbeat while encouraging women that the good stuff is worth fighting for. She is the creator of Adventures With Archer and the founder of Pursuit Community, a global movement helping women build successful businesses & thriving homes. Karen and her husband Isaac spend their days loving, adventuring, and forgiving with two tweens and a toddler on their Oregon farm.

Follow along with Karen at WWW.KARENSTOTT.COM

CHECK OUT THESE OTHER
JOURNALS FROM ADVENTURES WITH ARCHER

 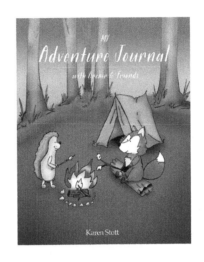

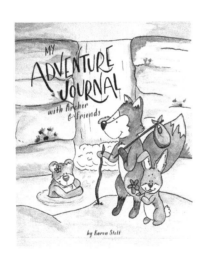 

AVAILABLE AT WWW.ADVENTURESWITHARCHER.COM

Made in the USA
Columbia, SC
29 March 2018